GET INTO ART

TELLING STORIES

SUSIE BROOKS

KINGFISHER

NEW YORK

KINGFISHER
LONDON & NEW YORK

Copyright © Kingfisher 2015
Published in the United States by Kingfisher,
175 Fifth Ave., New York, NY 10010
Kingfisher is an imprint of Macmillan Children's Books, London
All rights reserved.

Text and project material Copyright © Susie Brooks 2015

Distributed in the U.S. and Canada by Macmillan,
175 Fifth Ave., New York, NY 10010

Edited by Catherine Brereton and Polly Goodman
Designed by Peter Clayman
Cover design by Peter Clayman and Jane Tassie
Project photography by Peter Clayman
Picture research by AME Picture Research

Library of Congress Cataloging-in-Publication data
has been applied for.

ISBN 978-0-7534-7183-8

Kingfisher books are available for special promotions and premiums. For details contact:
Special Markets Department, Macmillan, 175 Fifth Ave., New York, NY 10010.

For more information, please visit www.kingfisherbooks.com

Printed in China
9 8 7 6 5 4 3 2 1
1TR/1114/LFG/UG/140MA

Picture credits
The Publisher would like to thank the following for permission to reproduce their material.
Every care has been taken to trace copyright holders. However, if there have been unintentional omissions or failure
to trace copyright holders, we apologize and will, if informed, endeavor to make corrections in any future edition.
Top = t; Bottom = b; Center = c; Left = l; Right = r
Cover and page 20 *Elizabeth I, Armada Portrait* by George Gower/Woburn Abbey, Bedfordshire, UK/The Bridgeman
Art Library; pages 4 and 8 *Homage to Blériot* by Robert Delaunay/The Art Archive/DeA Picture Library; 6 *William the
Conqueror's Fleet Crossing the English Channel, detail from the Bayeux Tapestry*/The Art Archive/DeA Picture Library;
10 *Illustration from Cinderella* by Arthur Rackham/The Art Archive/Kharbine-Tapabor; 12 *Automat* by Edward Hopper/The
Art Archive /DeA Picture Library; 14 *Noah's Ark stained glass window from Canterbury Cathedral*/The Art Archive/Kharbine-
Tapabor/Coll. Cowen; 16 *The Spinners* by Diego Velázquez/The Art Archive/Museo del Prado Madrid/Collection Dagli
Orti; 18 *Lone Dog's Winter Count* by Lone Dog/Corbis; 22 *Icarus* by Henri Matisse/Digital Image © 2014 Succession H.
Matisse/DACS 2014; 24 *The World Upside Down* by Jan Steen/The Art Archive/DeA Picture Library/G. Nimatallah;
26 *Niccolo Mauruzi da Tolentino at Battle of San Romano* by Paolo Uccello/The Art Archive/National Gallery London/Eileen
Tweedy; 28 *Dream of a Sunday Afternoon in Alameda Central Park* by Diego Rivera/© The Art Archive/Hotel del Prado
Mexico City/A. Dagli Orti © 2014 Banco de México Diego Rivera Frida Kahlo Museums Trust, Mexico, D.F./DACS; Paint
splatter motif throughout Shutterstock/RLN.

CONTENTS

PICTURE A STORY

What's your favorite story? The chances are that you have a picture of it in your mind! Many artists choose stories as their subjects, from imaginary tales to historical events or things that have happened in people's lives. Children's books are packed with illustrations, while other works of art show stories in a single scene. It's true that every picture tells a story in its own individual way!

See how stories have inspired famous artists—then **let them inspire you, too!** Each page of this book will tell you about a work of art and the person who created it. When you lift the flap, you'll find a project based on the artwork. Don't feel that you have to copy it exactly. Half the fun of art is exploring your own ideas!

GETTING STARTED

There's a checklist on page 31 that will tell you what you need for each project, but it's a good idea to read through the steps before you begin. There are also some handy tips on the next page . . .

Always have a **pencil** and **eraser** handy. Making a rough **sketch** can help you plan a project and see how it's going to look.

PICK YOUR PAINT...

Acrylic paints are thick and bright —they're great for strong colors, as well as textures such as grass.

Tempera paints are cheaper than acrylics but still bright. Use them when you need a lot of paint.

Watercolors give a thinner coloring that you can build up in layers, called washes.

Use a mixture of thick and thin **paintbrushes**. Have a glass jar or plastic cup of water ready to rinse them in and a **palette** or paper plate for mixing paint.

acrylic paint

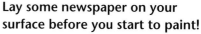

Lay some newspaper on your surface before you start to paint!

watercolor paint

sponged paint

TRY PASTELS ...

Oil pastels have a bright, waxy look, like crayons. **Soft pastels** can be smudged and blended like chalk.

oil pastels

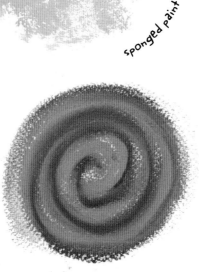
soft pastels

For painting, use thick **drawing** or **watercolor paper**—anything too thin will wrinkle. **Pastel paper** has a rough surface that holds on to the color.

Collect a range of **colored papers and cardboard** for collages and 3D models.

Ready to start? Let's **get into art!**

Look around at home for other art materials. Useful things include sponges, rags or cloths, scissors, string, glue, old packaging, plastic straws, felt or fabric, and tinfoil.

MARE

SEW A BOAT

Follow these steps **to stitch your own sailing scene!**

1 Using colorful felt or other strong fabric, cut out the shape of a boat and sail.

2 Thread a large needle with colored yarn and knot the end. On a spare piece of fabric, practice making stitches like these. If you haven't sewn before, ask an adult to help you.

This straight stitch is also called a running stitch.

Sew a row of running stitches, and then weave another color through the stitches.

Make a row of up-and-down stitches.

Sew diagonals to make Xs.

3 Use the stitches that you've learned to decorate the boat and sail with different colored yarn.

4 Stitch or glue your boat and sail onto another piece of fabric. Sew a mast and some wiggly lines for waves.

You could sew on some sailors, too.

Why not make a series of scenes and line them up like a cartoon strip!

WILLIAM THE CONQUEROR'S FLEET

Bayeux Tapestry 1000s

Imagine a cartoon strip that's three-fourths the size of a football field!
That's one way to describe the Bayeux Tapestry, which this sailing scene is a part of.

Sewn story

If you saw the whole Bayeux Tapestry, it might take you a while to find this boat—you'd have to search 230 feet (70 meters) of cloth decorated with 632 people, 202 horses, 560 other creatures, 41 ships, and a lot more! The pictures tell the story of William the Conqueror and his invasion of England more than 900 years ago.

This scene shows William's fleet crossing the English Channel from Normandy, France. They're on their way to victory at the Battle of Hastings. We can see the sails billowing on their wooden longboats, laden with horses, soldiers, and shields. Every tiny detail is sewn in woolen yarn on linen fabric. In fact, this type of stitching isn't called tapestry at all, but embroidery!

WHY WAS IT MADE?

The story on the Bayeux Tapestry is told from the invaders' point of view, so it was probably made as a celebration. We think that it was ordered by William's half brother, Bishop Odo of Bayeux. No one really knows who sewed it, but it might have been a group of nuns who were skilled at needlework.

SALUTE TO SPACE

Use Delaunay's colorful style **to make a tribute to modern space flight!**

1 On a piece of thick white paper, draw some space-inspired shapes. Think of swirling galaxies, planets, stars, moons, rockets, or even satellites—keep them simple!

Draw around circular objects, or use a compass.

2 Color in your shapes using oil pastels or crayons. The harder you press, the bolder the colors will be.

You can smudge colors together with your finger or a cloth.

3 Keep coloring until you've filled in the main shapes—leave the background blank.

4 Brush dark blue or black watercolor paint all over the background and any other gaps. The colored areas will resist the paint!

HOMAGE TO BLÉRIOT

Robert Delaunay 1914

In 1909, an exciting story hit the news —someone had flown a plane across the English Channel! A few years later, Robert Delaunay celebrated it on canvas.

Soaring shapes

Flying a plane from France to England might not be a big deal today, but Louis Blériot was the first person to do it! He won a prize of £1,000 and became a hero on both sides of the English Channel. Delaunay chose a rainbow of flight-inspired shapes to honor him.

Look at the circles—do they remind you of spinning propellers? There's a biplane soaring above the Eiffel Tower, but Blériot flew a monoplane with only one set of wings. Can you see it here? Delaunay didn't want to create a detailed, realistic scene. Instead, he painted bright, simple shapes that seem to whirl and flicker. They make us feel the energy and thrill of flying through the air!

WHO WAS DELAUNAY?

Robert Delaunay was born in France in 1885. He worked as a theater designer before becoming a painter. As an artist he was inspired by different modern styles, from Impressionism to Cubism and Expressionism. He blended them in his own colorful world of bold, often abstract shapes.

CHARACTER CUTOUTS

Choose a scene from your favorite fairy tale **and illustrate it with a silhouette!**

1 First practice drawing your characters on scrap paper. Show them from a side view, with the nose and arms sticking out. Just draw the outline —you won't see anything else in a silhouette.

You can exaggerate noses, chins, and hair for funny characters!

Think about their mood and what they're doing —a pose can say a lot.

2 When you're happy with a character, cut it out and place it face down on black paper. Draw around it in white pencil and cut it out.

Turn the cutout over so that you can't see any white lines.

3 Repeat step 2 for the other figures and features in your scene.

Include a couple of color details if you like!

4 Now arrange your cutouts on white paper or cardboard and glue them down. You could make a decorative border to finish off the picture!

Fold a strip of black paper back and forth like an accordion. Cut small shapes into the folds, and then open the paper out.

SCENE FROM CINDERELLA

Arthur Rackham 1919

You might recognize this scene from a folklore version of *Cinderella*. Rackham brings the famous story to life with his simple but magical illustrations.

Telling tails

Can you tell what's happening here? The fairy godmother is turning six lizards into footmen! We can see them changing little by little from animal to human—look at their tails getting shorter. They'll soon be ready to take Cinderella to the ball in her pumpkin carriage.

Of course, *Cinderella* is a made-up story, so no one really knows what the fairy godmother looked like. Rackham imagined her as a friendly, witchy character with a hooked nose and a pointy hat! He illustrated this scene and the rest of the book in a style called silhouette. He was excellent at showing poses and expressions through plain black shapes with very little detail within them.

WHO WAS RACKHAM?

Arthur Rackham was born in England in 1867. He grew up loving to draw, and later made his name as a great illustrator. Known for his imaginative characters and enchanted scenes, he decorated the pages of many famous books—from children's fairy tales to plays of Shakespeare!

SECRET STORY

Think up your own story **to illustrate in a mysterious scene!**

1 On a piece of colored pastel paper, sketch out a scene. Include a person, a light of some kind, and small details that make the viewer ask questions.

2 Using a bright yellow or white soft pastel, color the areas where the light is coming from.

3 Gradually color in the rest of the scene using colored pastels. You can blend colors together using your fingers.

End of a pastel

Side of a pastel

Two colors blended with a finger

4 Finish with strong, bright highlights and dark shadows. Then ask a friend to guess what's happening in your story!

Lighten the places that the light would be shining on.

Shadows fall away from the light.

AUTOMAT

Edward Hopper 1927

Some stories are imagined—and some make us do the imagining! In this painting, Hopper sets the scene for a story but leaves a sense of mystery dangling over it.

Puzzling picture

The painting makes us ask a lot of questions. Who is this woman? What is she doing here? Is she waiting for someone? What kind of mood is she in? She is well dressed and wearing makeup. Is she on her way to or from work or a party? Her clothes suggest that it's cold outside, but we can't tell from the dark sky whether it is early morning or night.

How long do you think the woman has been here? She's still wearing a glove, so perhaps she has only recently sat down. But we can also see an empty plate in front of her—has she had time for something to eat? Maybe she is thinking about leaving. There's no action to give away the full story. Hopper leaves it up to us to fill in the gaps!

WHO WAS HOPPER?

Edward Hopper was born in New York in 1882. He studied art and worked briefly as an illustrator before making his name as a painter. Hopper became famous for his quiet city scenes with isolated figures and dramatic lighting. Most of the women that he painted were modeled on his wife.

WINDOW WINGS

You can create the effect of stained glass **with some black paper and colored tissue paper.**

1 Fold a piece of letter-size (or larger) black paper in half. On one side, draw half of a butterfly using a white pencil or crayon. Cut it out, keeping the fold.

Folded edge is here.

2 With the paper still folded, draw on some simple shapes for markings. Leave a gap between them and around the edge. Carefully cut out the shapes.

Pinch the paper in the middle of a shape and cut a small slit. Then cut around the shape from the inside.

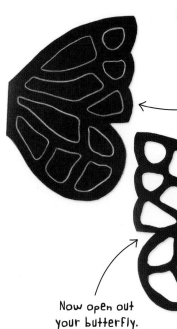

Now open out your butterfly.

3 Lay your butterfly pencil side up. Cut pieces of tissue paper a little bigger than the holes. Glue around the edges of the holes and stick the tissue paper down.

Do matching colors on each side.

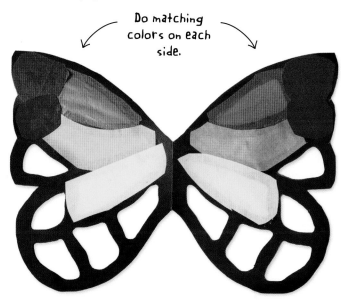

4 Turn your butterfly over and stick it to a window using adhesive putty. If you make another butterfly, they can fly to Noah's Ark two by two!

Stained glass is still used as an art form to tell stories, celebrate people's lives or events, or just decorate rooms with dancing patterns of light. You can see windows like this in churches, mosques, synagogues, and many other buildings—some people even have them in their homes! The way stained glass is made has barely changed since it was invented, though many more colors are available today.

NOAH'S ARK

Canterbury Cathedral 1200s

Windows aren't just for looking out of— sometimes they tell stories instead! This one, made of colorful stained glass, illustrates a scene from the Bible.

Seeing the light

The man we can see here is Noah. In the Bible story, he builds a giant ark to save his family and two of every type of animal from a terrible flood. One day he sends out a dove, which returns with an olive branch in its beak. This tells Noah that the flood is easing off and land is somewhere within reach.

Imagine this picture as part of a huge cathedral window packed with religious scenes. It was made at a time when few people were able to read, but they could learn a lot from the bright stained-glass images. As the sun moved around throughout the day, different windows would come alive like a colored light show. It must have been exciting long before movies or television were invented!

HOW WAS IT MADE?

The glass had to be melted and colored with chemicals before cooling and flattening out. Small details, such as faces and feathers, were painted on— often with a black pigment mixed with urine! The pieces were carefully cut to shape and then arranged and joined together with strips of lead.

SPINNING SPIDERS

Create the next scene in Arachne's story **by showing her as a spider spinning webs!**

1 On a piece of stiff cardboard, draw a spider web. Keep it simple—too many lines will make it difficult to print.

Draw the diagonal lines first.

2 Starting with the diagonals again, cut pieces of thick string or cord to the length of the lines. Cover each line with strong craft glue and stick the string down.

3 When the glue is dry, squeeze some white paint onto a paper plate. Use a sponge to cover the web in paint, and then press it firmly down onto a sheet of colored paper.

When you lift off the cardboard, you'll find a print!

4 Take a large piece of colored paper and print several webs by repeating step 3. Then dip your thumb in black paint to print some spiders. Paint on eyes and draw the legs with a felt-tip pen or marker.

You can print extra lines using the edge of a piece of cardboard.

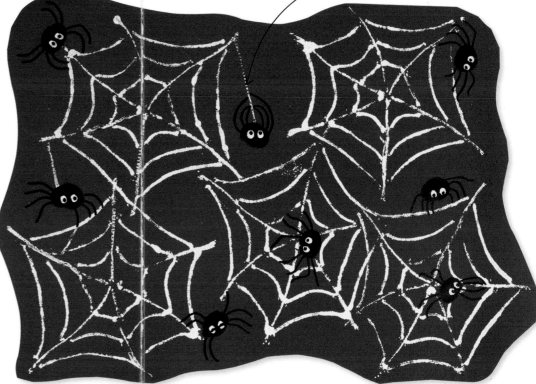

THE SPINNERS

Diego Velázquez, *about* 1657

This large painting tells a story in two parts. It begins in the foreground, close to the viewer, and then continues at the back of the scene.

Weaving a tale

Velázquez chose a Greek myth, the fable of Arachne, as the subject of his painting. It tells of a peasant girl named Arachne who challenged the goddess Athena to a weaving contest. When Arachne produced a tapestry as beautiful as Athena's, the goddess became angry—and turned the poor girl into a spider!

Athena is the figure in the headscarf, while Arachne has her back to us on the right. They are busy spinning yarn for their work. Velázquez arranged them carefully, leading our eye slowly toward the lit-up back room where Arachne's finished tapestry hangs on the wall. We can see Athena in a helmet in front of it, raising her arm in fury. Velázquez expects us to know what happens next!

WHO WAS VELÁZQUEZ?

Diego Velázquez was born in Spain in 1599. At the age of 11, he became apprenticed to a local painter who recognized his artistic talent. Later he was made court painter to King Philip IV and lived in the royal palace. He also traveled to Italy, where other great artists influenced his work.

WHAT COUNTS?

Illustrate your own life story **in the style of a winter count!**

1 First prepare your background. Scrunch up a big piece of thick white paper, and then open it out again. Soak a few black tea bags in warm water and squeeze and dab them over the paper. Leave to dry.

The more tea you use, the darker the effect will be.

2 Now write a list of things that you remember from different times in your life. Think of at least 20 if you can. For each one, design your own special symbol. Here are a few examples:

Think about birthdays, family events, vacations, school field trips, and other activities.

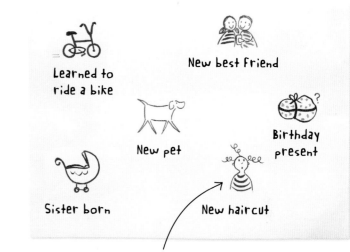

Learned to ride a bike

New best friend

New pet

Birthday present

Sister born

New haircut

Make the symbols as simple or as colorful as you like!

3 Tear a rough edge around the paper to make it look like a buffalo hide. Then draw or paint your symbols in the order that they happened.

Start in the middle and work in a spiral, turning the paper as you go.

If you leave some space, you can keep adding to your life-story picture!

Day at the movies

Great party!

Long trip

Getting into art!

LONE DOG'S WINTER COUNT

Lone Dog 1800–1870

Here's a story that you read from the inside out!
Each symbol in this spiral represents a year in the life of the Native American Yanktonai Nakota people.

Dates to remember
We may use dates in our diaries, but Lone Dog and others used pictures instead. Every year, they chose the most memorable thing that had happened and drew a symbol, or pictograph, for it. This built up a decorative record of their history —there are 70 years shown here.

Try to find the following: a spotted figure (many people died of smallpox), a lasso (wild horses were caught), two hands about to shake (a peace agreement), a black Sun (solar eclipse). Other events include trading with Europeans, battles with other tribes, floods, pony thefts, and a meteor shower. They're all drawn on a buffalo skin, or hide.

WHY A WINTER COUNT?

It's called a winter count because the Nakota measured their years between each first snowfall. Every year, the elders met to decide on the event to record. As time passed, the keeper of the count had to remember what his symbols meant so that he could tell the stories to others!

DRESSING UP

Imagine you're part of a royal family—**design yourself a costume as grand as Queen Elizabeth's!**

Print your own "fabrics" by painting different objects and then pressing them onto paper.

Princess dress

End of a pencil

Pieces of a cupcake case or doily make great collars and cuffs!

Leaf

Rim of a pen lid or bottle cap

Edge of a strip of cardboard

Prince's pajamas

Cut triangle or rectangle shapes from a potato and use them to print patterns.

Roll up a narrow strip of paper for a button.

Royal robe

Print with half an onion or a section of cabbage.

Scrape patterns into wet acrylic paint.

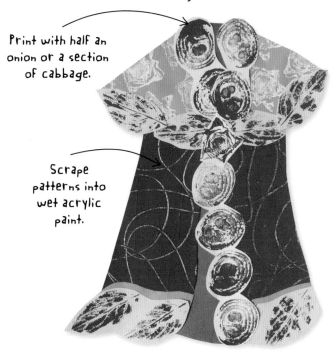

Crown

Twist pieces of tinfoil into decorative shapes.

Try sticking on gems or sequins.

You could draw or paint a picture of yourself in the costume—and add things in the background that say a little about you and your hobbies!

THE ARMADA PORTRAIT

Probably George Gower, *about* 1588

Every person has a story— and Elizabeth I of England's was an impressive one! This painting is more than just a portrait of the powerful and popular queen.

Glory story

In the year that this picture was painted, the British defeated an invasion from Spain known as the Spanish Armada. We can see two scenes from the battle in the background, on each side of the queen. Under her hand is a globe, a symbol of the power that she held in the world. Her clothes and jewels tell us that she was rich and grand.

In fact, this visual story has a few fibs in it, too. In 1588, Elizabeth was 55 years old and had wrinkled skin, black teeth, narrow lips, and thinning hair! This wasn't the image she wanted people to remember, so she ordered the artist to show her as an ageless beauty surrounded by wealth and glory.

WHO WAS GOWER?

This picture isn't signed by George Gower, but it seems likely that he painted it. Born in England around 1540, he became "serjeant painter" to Queen Elizabeth in 1581. His main job was to create portraits of the royals, but he also painted decorations on their furniture, palaces, and carriages.

FLYING WITHOUT WINGS

Cut out bold, bright shapes in the style of Matisse for this swirling Icarus mobile!

1 On a piece of dark-colored cardboard, draw a falling figure. Keep it simple—you don't have to draw hands or feet. Cut it out, and then draw around it on another piece of cardboard and cut that out, too.

You'll have a matching pair!

3 Cut out a large circle of blue cardboard, and then cut it into a spiral as shown. Use a needle to push a piece of yarn or thread through the center of the spiral to hang it up.

Knot the end of the thread so it doesn't slip through.

When Matisse created this picture, he was old and unwell, and his eyesight was failing. He worked by painting large sheets of paper and then cutting them into shapes—a method he called "drawing with scissors." In 1947, Matisse published a book called *Jazz* that was full of these colorful cutouts. On some of the pages he included handwritten notes and thoughts.

2 Cut out a round Sun and a few spark and feather shapes. Make a matching pair for each, as before. To hang the shapes, tape on a piece of thread, and then glue the matching pair over the top.

Do the same with your Icarus figure.

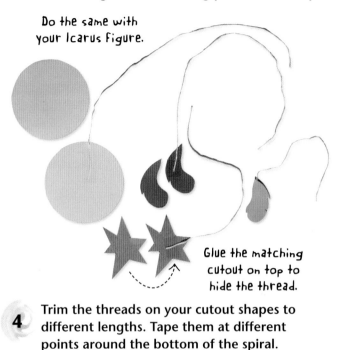

Glue the matching cutout on top to hide the thread.

4 Trim the threads on your cutout shapes to different lengths. Tape them at different points around the bottom of the spiral. Now you can hang up your mobile!

ICARUS

Henri Matisse 1943

Sometimes stories can be told in the simplest of pictures! Matisse illustrated this mythological tale using just a few colors and shapes.

Forever falling

It's never a good idea to fly close to the Sun when you're wearing wings made of feathers and wax! Icarus, a character from Greek mythology, found that out the hard way when his homemade wings melted, sending him plummeting into the sea.

In Matisse's picture we see Icarus falling, his head tilted as if he's looking down below. The brilliant blue sky is filled with flashes of yellow that remind us of blazing sunlight. Icarus was an adventurer, and his brave heart glows red in his chest. The simple shapes and curves make the fall seem graceful, like a dance—but the heavy black of the figure suggests that this will not end well.

WHO WAS MATISSE?

Matisse was born in France in 1869. He trained as a lawyer, but at the age of 20 he fell ill with appendicitis. His mother gave him a paint set to help him pass the time, and that's when his love of art began. Matisse became very famous, creating paintings, drawings, prints, collages, and sculptures. Some of his works have sold for more than $30 million!

SILLY STREET

Turn the world upside down, inside out, and topsy-turvy in a crazy collage!

1 Think of an ordinary, everyday setting such as a street, room, or school playground. Make a sketch of it, but fill it with a lot of strange or funny details.

Clothes standing on the line?

It's raining upward!

Hat feathers for a nest!

Where are his shoes?

Look out—there's a hole!

3 Look around for old magazines and scraps of patterned paper. Cut out shapes for the details in your picture and glue them down. Work from the background forward.

Try pictures of fur, wool, or carpet for animals and pictures of feathers for birds.

See if a friend can spot all of the things that are wrong!

2 Use a large piece of paper or posterboard for your collage. Start by cutting out and sticking down the main background features, as shown.

Weird—the sky's green!

Cut face shapes from skin-colored paper and hairstyles from hair photos.

WORLD UPSIDE DOWN

Jan Steen, *about* 1665

The world isn't actually upside down in this painting—but it isn't quite how it should be. Steen has woven in all sorts of little stories that tip ordinary life on its head!

Rowdy room

What do you see when you look at this household? Is there anything that seems a little strange? Maybe it's the boy smoking a pipe, the lady asleep at the table, or the dog chowing down on her dinner! No one seems to notice the baby throwing her food and playing with an expensive necklace. There's an indoor pig, a duck on a guest, and a monkey playing with a clock!

Jan Steen had a sense of humor. He loved to make jokes about the ordered lifestyles of people in the villages around him. While other Dutch artists painted prim and proper families in well-kept homes, Steen showed children with grownup bad habits and adults goofing off like kids!

WHO WAS STEEN?

Jan Steen was born in Holland in 1625 or 1626. He came from a family of brewers, and his paintings told stories of the everyday life around him. Often he included witty proverbs, or messages, in his work. *World Upside Down* is also known as *Beware of Luxury*—a warning about the penalties of being rich!

BATTLE IN A BOX

Play with space like Uccello and **create a 3D scene, or diorama, in a box!**

1 You'll need a large shoebox or something similar. Cut a piece of paper the same size as the box base and paint or stick on a simple landscape. Glue it inside the box.

You could decorate the sides of the box, too.

2 Practice sketching a rearing horse and rider, and then draw it onto thin cardboard. Then cut out the shape, leaving some extra cardboard at the bottom to make a flap.

Use these red lines as a guide for drawing the horse.

Draw a rock behind the back legs so you don't have to cut them out.

3 Turn your horse face down on some more cardboard, draw around it, and cut it out. Paint or decorate the figures, facing opposite ways. Fold back the flaps to make them stand.

Try sticking on yarn for reins, a feather on a helmet, and spears cut from plastic straws or cardboard.

4 Make as many horsemen as you like. Then arrange your battle scene in the box!

Why not cut out some swords and shields to scatter on the ground.

THE BATTLE
OF SAN ROMANO

Paolo Uccello, *about* 1438–1440

The good thing about painting a battle story is you can pick the parts you show!
Uccello chose glory over gory in this enormous picture, painted for a family on the winning side.

A beautiful battle

In real life, Uccello's painting is 10 feet (3 meters) wide! It tells the story of a battle between the Italian cities of Florence and Sienna. Can you guess who is leading the victorious Florentine side? Of course it's the man on the white horse! He's Niccolò da Tolentino, and he's the first thing we notice in the scene.

Uccello has ignored a lot of the reality of battle. His hero doesn't even wear a helmet to protect his head. Instead, we see decorative costumes, beautiful scenery, and a crisscross pattern of scattered swords. Uccello had just discovered the technique of perspective, which gave his painting a 3D feel. Apparently, he would stay up all night trying to get the angles exactly right!

WHO WAS UCCELLO?

Paolo di Dono was born in Italy in 1397. ("Uccello" was really a nickname, given for his love of painting birds.) He became apprenticed to a sculptor at the age of ten, and then turned to painting in his teens. This picture, one of three that he made of the same battle, is one of his most famous works.

UP AND AWAY!

Rivera made his paintings on fresh plaster. **You can create a similar effect on modeling clay.**

1 Roll out a block of air-dry modeling clay until it's about half an inch (1.25 cm) thick. Use the end of a paintbrush to pierce two holes right through the clay near the top. Let it dry overnight.

You can neaten up the edges with a knife or leave them rough.

3 When you're happy with your outline, use acrylic or tempera paints to color it in. Let the painting dry.

2 Now think up a story based on a hot-air balloon—it could be a little wacky, like a dream! Where is it going? Who's onboard? When your clay is dry, draw on a scene in pencil.

No one will get their hands on this flying pirate's treasure!

4 Thread a piece of string through the holes and knot the ends together at the back. You can now hang your picture on a wall!

DREAM OF A SUNDAY AFTERNOON IN ALAMEDA CENTRAL PARK

Diego Rivera 1947

Sometimes the strangest stories happen in our dreams! In this dreamlike painting, Rivera takes a walk in the park with hundreds of characters from history.

Distant memories

The boy in striped socks is the artist himself, aged ten, with a frog and snake in his pockets. He holds hands with a living skeleton woman dressed in a fancy plumed hat. Skeleton characters were a speciality of the artist José Guadalupe Posada, who stands on her other side. Behind the young Rivera we can also see Frida Kahlo, his future wife.

This is just a section of Rivera's huge picture, which he painted on a hotel wall. He mixed his own memories with the story of his home country, Mexico. While some scenes seem like the stuff of nightmares, the hot-air balloon is a symbol of hope. It's decorated with the colors of the Mexican flag and "RM" for *República Mexicana.*

WHO WAS RIVERA?

Diego Rivera was born in Mexico in 1886. Even as a boy he loved drawing on walls, so no wonder he became famous for his murals! Rivera liked to paint scenes with messages that often shocked other people. He created huge public pictures so that everyone could see what he believed in.

ART WORDS AND INFO

abstract Not representing an actual object, place, or living thing. Abstract art often focuses on simplified shapes, lines, colors, or use of space.

apprentice Someone who works for an employer in order to learn a certain skill.

canvas A strong type of fabric on which artists can paint or sew designs.

collage A picture made by sticking pieces of paper, fabric, or other objects onto a surface.

court painter An artist who painted for a royal or noble family, often agreeing not to take on other work.

Cubism (1907–1920s) An art style that involved making images using simple geometric shapes.

embroidery The art of decorating fabric with stitched designs in yarn or thread.

Expressionism (1905–1920s) An art style that was about feelings and emotions, often shown through distorted shapes or colors.

foreground The part of a picture or scene that appears closest to the viewer.

illustrator An artist who creates illustrations—pictures that explain or decorate a story or other piece of writing.

Impressionism (1870s–1890s) An art style that focused on color and the changing effects of light. Impressionist artists often painted outdoors and tried to capture passing moments.

landscape A scene or painting of a scene, usually in the countryside.

mural A picture painted on a wall.

mythological Relating to myths—traditional stories told by ancient cultures such as the ancient Greeks.

COLOR CONNECTIONS

In art there are three primary colors—**red, yellow,** and **blue**. These are colors that can't be mixed from any others. Each primary color has an opposite color, or complementary color, which is made by mixing the other two primary colors.

If you mix a color with its complementary color, you'll get a shade of brown.

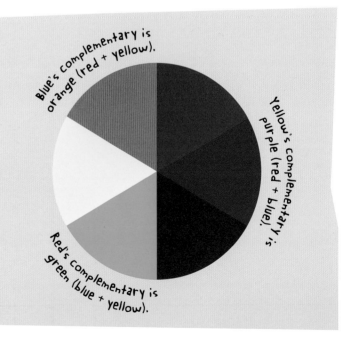

Blue's complementary is orange (red + yellow).

Yellow's complementary is purple (red + blue).

Red's complementary is green (blue + yellow).

perspective The art of showing three-dimensional objects on a flat page, creating the effect of depth or distance.

portrait A painting, sculpture, or other artwork that shows an image of a particular person.

print A way of transferring an image from one surface to another. Prints are often made by spreading ink over a raised or engraved design and then pressing it onto paper. This makes a reverse image that can be reproduced many times.

proverb A short, popular saying that contains a message or piece of advice.

sculptor An artist who makes three-dimensional art, called sculpture. Carving and clay modeling are types of sculpture.

serjeant painter A highly honored artist employed by the British royal household.

silhouette A picture of something that shows the shape and outline only, usually colored in black.

sketch A rough drawing or painting, often made to help plan a final artwork.

symbol A shape or icon that stands for, or represents, something else.

tapestry The art of weaving designs in yarn or thread onto a stiff cloth or canvas.

texture The feel of a surface, such as rough brick or smooth glass.

three-dimensional (3D) Describes something that has height, width, and depth.

PROJECT CHECKLIST

Below is a list of materials that you'll need for each project in this book. The ones in parentheses are useful, but you can manage without them!

Sew a boat (page 7) colorful felt or other strong fabric, scissors, different colored yarn, large needle, glue

Salute to space (page 9) thick white paper, pencil, eraser, round objects or compass, oil pastels or crayons, watercolor paint, paintbrush, (cloth)

Character cutouts (page 11) scrap paper, pen or pencil, scissors, black paper, white pencil, glue, white paper, (colored paper)

Secret story (page 13) colored pastel paper, pencil, eraser, soft pastels

Window wings (page 15) letter-size or larger black paper, white pencil or crayon, scissors, colored tissue paper, glue, adhesive putty

Spinning spiders (page 17) stiff cardboard, pen or pencil, thick string or cord, scissors, strong craft glue, white paint, paper plate, colored paper, black paint, black felt-tip pen or marker

What counts? (page 19) thick white paper, tea bags, pencil, felt-tip pens, crayons or paints and paintbrush

Dressing up (page 21) colored paper, scissors, glue, paints, paper plate or palette, pencil, pen lid or bottle cap, leaves, strip of cardboard, potato, onion or cabbage, tinfoil, (gems or sequins)

Flying without wings (page 23) colored cardboard, pencil, scissors, thread, needle, tape

Silly street (page 25) drawing paper or posterboard, pencil, eraser, colored paper, scissors, glue, old magazines, scraps of patterned paper

Battle in a box (page 27) large shoebox, paper, scissors, paints, paintbrush, glue, thin cardboard, (yarn, feathers, plastic straws, shiny paper)

Up and away! (page 29) air-dry modeling clay, paintbrush, pencil, acrylic or tempera paints, string, scissors

INDEX